Wali Dad's Gifts

by Carl Murano
illustrated by Stephen Costanza

 ## HOUGHTON MIFFLIN HARCOURT
School Publishers

Printed in China

ISBN-13: 978-0-547-02170-6
ISBN-10: 0-547-02170-4

2 3 4 5 6 7 8 0940 18 17 16 15 14 13 12 11 10

Once upon a time there lived a man named Wali Dad. He lived in a mud hut far from the village. He worked as a grass-cutter—cutting grass and selling it in the marketplace as food for horses.

This work did not pay much, but it was enough for Wali Dad to live on. He was a simple man, and he lived a simple life. After he bought food and clothing, he saved the rest of his earnings in a clay pot he kept under his bed.

Wali Dad lived this way for many years. One night he decided to count the coins he had saved. He pulled out the clay pot. He was startled to see that the pot contained hundreds of coins.

"What will I do with all this money? I have everything I need. I need nothing more," thought Wali Dad. Then suddenly he had an idea. Wali Dad went to sleep, ready to act on his plan in the morning.

At sunrise Wali Dad tossed the coins into a pouch. He traveled to the marketplace and began to search for the jeweler's stall. In exchange for all his coins, Wali Dad bought a beautiful gold bracelet from the jeweler.

Next, Wali Dad went to the home of a traveling merchant. He asked the merchant, "Who is the finest lady in all the world?"

The merchant replied, "That would be the princess who lives three days' journey to the east. I often travel to her palace to buy and sell goods."

Wali Dad pulled out the bracelet. "As a favor, would you kindly present the princess with this bracelet? Please tell her that Wali Dad has sent it."

The merchant agreed to do as Wali Dad asked. The next time he was at the princess's palace, he gave her the bracelet as a gift from Wali Dad.

The princess was quite pleased with the bracelet, but she insisted on sending Wali Dad a gift in return. And so the merchant was sent off with packages of fine silks for Wali Dad.

Wali Dad was surprised by the gift of silks. In his simple life, he had no use for such riches. Then a thought struck him. He asked the merchant, "Who is the finest man in all the world?"

The merchant replied, "That would be the prince who lives three days' journey to the west. I have been to his palace many times to buy and sell goods."

Wali Dad said, "Please do me another favor. Give these silks to the prince as a gift from Wali Dad."

The merchant agreed and set off once again. The prince was pleased with the silks, but he insisted on sending Wali Dad a gift in return. And so he sent the merchant off with twelve splendid horses for Wali Dad.

"Oh no!" cried Wali Dad when the merchant presented the horses. "In my simple life, what can I do with twelve horses?"

Then Wali Dad thought of a solution. He said to the merchant, "Please keep two of the horses for yourself. Take the rest to the princess."

The merchant agreed and set off once again.

Now the princess wanted to stop Wali Dad from sending more gifts. So she sent a gift she was sure could never be matched. She sent twenty mules loaded with silver.

Wali Dad had no intention of keeping the mules and the silver, but again he had a solution. He gave two mules and their silver to the merchant. He pleaded with the merchant to take the rest to the prince.

By now, the merchant knew the routine, and he hurried to the prince's palace with the mules and the silver. The prince wanted to stop Wali Dad's gifts, too. So he sent a gift he was sure could never be matched. He sent horses, camels, and elephants.

As in the past, the riches dismayed Wali Dad. He begged the merchant to keep two of each animal and take the rest to the princess.

The merchant felt odd about continuing as Wali Dad's messenger. But he agreed to go one more time. He delivered the horses, camels, and elephants to the princess.

Now the princess wanted to meet Wali Dad. She felt his gifts signaled his wish to marry her. She asked the merchant to inform Wali Dad of her visit.

Upon hearing of the princess's visit, Wali Dad became upset. "How can I welcome the princess to my simple hut?" he asked.

The merchant had no answer.

"Then I must leave my home," Wali Dad said.

The next morning, Wali Dad left his hut. He leaned against the door one last time. Then he started down the road. He had to leave his old life behind.

As Wali Dad walked down the road, he saw two women dressed in golden robes.

"Why are you leaving your home?" they asked.

Wali Dad told the women the story of the gifts. He told them how he could not welcome the princess to his humble hut. He explained that the only solution was for him to leave his home.

The two women did not agree. They turned Wali Dad's old clothes into a brand-new suit. They turned his mud hut into a palace.

Just then the princess arrived from the east. And the prince arrived from the west, as he wanted to meet the giver of the gifts, too.

When the princess and prince met, they fell in love. They planned to marry.

The next morning, Wali Dad left his palace and started down the road. Before he had gone too far, the two women in golden robes appeared again.

"Where are you going?" they asked.

Wali Dad answered, "I am grateful for what I have been given, but I am a simple man. I want to live a simple life."

At that, the women returned Wali Dad's old clothes and his mud hut. Wali Dad went back to grass-cutting. And although he thought often of the princess and the prince, he never sent them another gift again.